MODERN AND NORMAL

MODERN AND NORMAL

KAREN SOLIE

Brick Books

Library and Archives Canada Cataloguing in Publication

Solie, Karen, 1966-
    Modern and normal / Karen Solie.

Poems.
ISBN 1-894078-47-0

I. Title.

PS8587.O4183M63 2005   C811'.54   C2005-903457-2

We acknowledge the support of the Canada Council for the Arts, the Government of Canada through the Book Publishing Industry Development Program (BPIDP), and the Ontario Arts Council for their support of our publishing program.

The book is set in Helvetica and Minion

Design and layout by Alan Siu.

Printed by Sunville Printco Inc.

Brick Books
431 Boler Road, Box 20081
London, Ontario N6K 4G6

www.brickbooks.ca

Brick Books 1975–2005

For David Seymour

dwell, intr. v. – ME. *dwellen*, fr. OE. *dwellan*, 'to lead astray, deceive; to hinder; to wander, go astray; to tarry', rel. to ON. *dvelja*, 'to delay; to tarry', OHG. *twaljan*, 'to hinder, delay', OE. *dwolian*, 'to stray, err', *dwala, dwela, gedwola*, 'error', *gedwelan*, 'to err', and to E. **dull, dwale** (qq.v.) For the sense development of E. *dwell* (fr. OE. *dwellan*, 'to tarry'), cp. F. *demeurer*, 'to remain, stay, lodge, reside, live'.

— *Klein's Comprehensive Etymological Dictionary*

Contents

EVERYTHING'S OKAY

MORE OR LESS

Found

One Easy Lesson

> The sight picture, the way you lay the front post in the rear notch, is a part of the story but it is just stuff that acts as trimming. Unimportant. Of little consequence, that is compared to the Really Big Thing we are building up to.
>
> — Lt. Col. Charles Askins. From *Shooter's Bible Treasury*, New 2nd Ed., 1970 (originally published in the *Stoeger Catalogue* Edition No. 46, 1955)

The poor, benighted hombre who buys a onehand
shooting iron and thereafter looks about for advice
as to how to hit with it is really asking
for trouble! Advice about how to be a pistol whiz
is like all other kinds of counsel, it is free
and ofttimes misleading. Whether he simply talks
to the next man on the firing line, buys a book
and peruses it, or writes to the nearest firearms
editor, he is apt to wind up confused
and saddened. The woods are full of gents
who are pistol coaches, self-annointed.
Maybe they have never killed so much
as a cottontail, never punched out a possible
at any range, never were guilty of a single original
thought in the somewhat involved gymnastics
of sixgun juggling but they don't hesitate
to pop off. And especially to the poor innocent
who has just bought his first hardware. "Naw-naw.
Don't stand like that! Get your feet farther apart.
Put your hand in your pocket. See. Look at me. This
is the way!" The expert is correcting. The neophyte
is sweating. Or maybe he isn't such a recruit anymore.
Possibly he has burned up a few thousand rounds
and his problems have really grown complex.

More Fun in the New World

I lied about the shortcut, the high road,
all of it. Steered through the same recreational districts
dry-eyed and frostbit, as if on rails, and pulled up
just like that. Eight yards to the motel office, one more
to ring the bell. The ice machine means well, a grey slab
I attend with my bucket. I've been here before,
paced it off and slept beneath a sheet
forty feet from the highway. Darling,
they're tearing up the highway. When I said so long
I meant that I don't understand modern manners or the solar system
or anything. That a crucial lesson
didn't take. The new math ruined a generation. Just look
what we count on: blink of binary
operations. On check-in I find hair in the drain, a ring
by the phone, as though I'm late. Too late. At check-out
I buy more time for the purpose of making suspiciously
little noise, unable to believe a mid-sized Canadian airport
the last place I will ever see you. Come back. I'm low
on cash, downgrading, looking
at what poverty means to show me. This bed,
burned by cigarettes. The chair beside it.

You Never Know

The place has all the charm of a lost
wallet. Of getting used to the way things are now
and what you're known for. It wants a hammer,
a mouthful of nails, a good going-over
with bleach. Its tabs gallop headlong for yonder
horizon. A certain age, you've grown fond
of drinking among repairs forever
in the offing, alongside regulars sidelong
as perennial suspects whose kindnesses
and bouts of community service
have been deemed, again and again,
inadmissible. Don't ask. The air this night
of the first spring melt is germy and contingent.

And then what. You've seen it all
until everything forsworn, some gorgeous
hitch, drifts in like a front, blows you down
like a barn. No matter
that your bush league crime sprees, elopements
and artistic retreats all end in the same cheap
Niagara Falls motel room with a case of the jumps
and a wan motto: no one was supposed
to get hurt. Because we do. And turn up sooner
or later just like you, in a tip like this
on the wrong side of suppertime, a gamer,
and the rest of your life before you. No really.

Possibility

A rented late-model car. Strewn gear. Clothes,
books, liquor, one good knife for slicing
limes. Motel the orange of an old rind, bud green
and remaindered blue for trim. Some schemes

shouldn't work, but do. A square room
with balcony two floors above the strip. Real
keys. A man sleeping on the bed,
or pretending to. It will be all right. It's not

too late. We left on the sly and nothing bad
happened. Every desire ponied up, in fact,
down to the nod, as though our due. We used
them well, and barely ate. The roads

are there. The rooms, the bars, the manic
distractions and sublime yaw of geographical events
are there. Pricked by a whim, we blew town
with something like intent. It's hard to say.

On the fourth day we repacked
and drove back in.

Cardio Room, Young Women's Christian Association

You won't know me. Any resemblance
to the woman I was is purely
agricultural. That fluff. A pink annual
given to low-born intemperate acts
unbecoming a modern person. No more.
I'm tough. Nothing
could eat me. No profligate billy
with a hacking cough, or that old goat
and his yen for plagues, floods, and burning
fun places to the ground. Not you,
either. There was a time
I rolled like dough, plumped up
to be thumped down with artless yeasty
chemistry. Dumpling. Honeybun.
I sickened some. But evolved
in a flash, like the living flak
of a nuclear mistake. In space-age fabrics
I've moved more iron than a red
blood cell, climbing and climbing
the new world's dumbest tower. I'm on
to this. Alongside the rest
I sweat it out with the smug one-party
affability of a sport utility
vehicle. Deceptively little cargo space.
Even covered in mud I look great.

One Night Stand

I could say it's a wash
in a border town where even the border
is at sea. On a clear day,
America bellies up in plain sight
across the blameless strait. I could say
constancy's a dodgy topic,
though I've been years in a house
that suits me well enough,
with its doorknobs and its doors,
and I'm known in certain corners
as a real live wire, tireless booster
of the last one standing. That night,
nothing but time. The bar
shucked bass into the street,
an unknown band from way down
east. He saw me from the stage
in my next-best dress. I was neither
here nor there. He drove through
2000 miles of rain, he said,
only to find me at the continent's
end. His gift to me. And mine to him
that I would not think of him again.

Larking

What swimmers. We cannot leave lie
any excuse to pitch into the drink. Nights,
as our lifeguards sleep, but nooners too,
and tea time. A dip first thing will goose

the blood up. The grounded are a bore.
They toss inflatables out from shore,
trot home to call their friends: *yes
old so-and-so's in headfirst again.*

And we are buoyant for a spell. Until
sogged, we emerge heartbroken, skint,
or just made fool of, prone to fever or the itch,
and must dry out. Those landlocked stints

a rocky province, grimly lit
with no high ground to recommend it.

Found

Bruce. After Last Call

— Overheard. Thursday's Bar, Victoria, Feb, 2000

It was fun. Got us out of Lethbridge.
We used to drive to Raymond
to beat up their quarterback.
They have the highest rate of injury. Short,
usually. My girlfriend Leslie was a sweet
Mormon princess. She left me
for the big man. First time I met him
he patted me on the head and said
"You're a good football player."
I spent four years with the NCAA, brought in
as centre. They liked my attitude and ability
to buy weed. If there're 24 jobs in the NFL
there are 34,000 players applying
for each one. You'd never think it.
I'm a little guy now. Coke. Booze.
Steroids. We dropped acid
and went to the dinosaur museum
in Pocatello, Idaho. Otherwise, lots of guns
and buying drugs from Hawaiians.
If there was an asshole alive,
I knew him. People think all jocks
are fucked. I've spent years apologizing
to my mother for the porcupine incident.

Nice

"I think I'm kind of two-faced. I'm very ingratiating. It
really kind of annoys me. I'm just sort of a little too
nice. Everything is Oooo."

— Diane Arbus

Still dark, but just. The alarm
kicks on. A voice like a nice hairdo
squeaks *People, get ready*
for another nice one. Low 20s,
soft breeze, ridge of high pressure
settling nicely. Songbirds swallowing, ruffling,
starting in. Does anyone curse
the winter wren, calling in Christ's name
for just one bloody minute of silence?
Of course not. They sound nice.
I pull away and he asks why I can't
be nicer to him. Well,
I have to work, I say, and wouldn't it be nice
if someone made some money today?
Very nice, he quavers, rolling
his face to the wall. A nice face.
A nice wall. We agreed on the green
down to hue and shade straight away.
That was a very nice day.

Pacific Daylight Time

Spring ahead, fall back. It all works out.
Like it or not the world turns and sometimes you lose
an hour, forced to smoke outside while the band plays.
Not a good band, but it plays. Streetlights spit, pop,
and blank. Cab fare: spent. Someone
will come along. We circle in
like cows against the wind, on one foot,

then the next.
Across the street, a house on sale for years, a joke,
a junkie roost, sign trashed, flapping, and next to it,
a store for orthotics, prosthetics, all the props
of aging. Cars slash through seasonal rain,
wipers on. Again, again.
If it's important it's under construction. Like magic,

really, how things get done.
We will go home and wait for calls. Someone
must wonder where we are. Next door,
the Baptist church's sign, magnetic, illuminated,
knifes a psalm, Hebrews,
through this lousy weather: *Jesus Christ
is the same yesterday, today, and forever.*

Watch Your Head

So what? I tried. So what. Retained the use of my hands,
a Scandinavian appreciation for the well-executed
blindside, and the rest came back gradually. I haven't
learned a thing. Like the man who thought a drive would do
him good; the row had been dreadful. Instead of sticking
to the straightaway he turned left and fell in love
with a barmaid at the Keno parlour in Morinville.
Or the one, down seven bills to a Tompkins VLT,
who slunk out to get the gun, returned, and with a muttered
stand aside, sighting clean on the display, shot
the fiend to shit. Who sank into a chair, then, double-barrel
on his lap, and waited out the cops as his cronies
gathered round the wreck trailing their own criminal
pasts, hissing *Way to go, Stan. Way to go.*

Trust Me

A drowning dream. Look up. Sunlight snickers
on the swells as fingers trail a calm
and vicious scratch across the surface
of an unsung lake and a boat rocks like a bed,
away. You know there's a town nearby,
but that it's dank and full of felons bent
on some shady holiday. Wake up. The ceiling
is awash with daylight chunnelling through the blinds.

Streetcars ride thin rails across the grid, noise
and indecision at the stops. When to get on. When
to get off. How much time there is to kill
and how much money is enough. Wise up to the rule.
It's fierce, squatting on the track between *yes,
of course I will* and *you fool, you fool.*

To Have and Have Not

To have missed the plane. To have never fit his body
to his name, felt them click, and that slip-knot below her navel
slip. To have not taken his hand, in a strange city,
and been overcome. To have reconsidered,
and meant it. To have not returned, those missing hours
presented like a bad meal, and thought that this
is how it feels to follow night across the world.
To have not lived inside it since. Oh to have taken
the guidance counsellor's advice and become a secretary.
To have done the right thing, or the wrong one,
but with conviction. To have never read *Eros and Civilization*
and developed a theory. To have asked questions first,
or none at all. To have never gone with him to the basement
and felt his mouth upon her skin. To have worn
not what she did but instead the blouse, the white one,
that with a touch falls away. To have not felt that slip-knot
slip, his body click, placed her hand upon his hip,
and been pushed up hard against the wall.

Untitled

You're still young. Someone curled an arm around you as you slept,
and upon awaking gently touched your face. The first sound you heard

today was a bird, a note of origin, before traffic. It's been years
since you thought the morning kind. Someone curled an arm around you

as you slept, and in the afternoon reached a hand toward you that you held,
simply. A note of origin, before traffic. Words you'd left behind rose

like birds to all they keep unto themselves. This is mine. Upon awaking
to that first sound, someone gently touched my face. This afternoon

I took his hand, simply, and reached across the words I'd left behind.
I'm still young. It's been years since I thought the morning kind.

Three in the Afternoon

Look, there's something
you ought to know. This room
and you in it is what
you have. Imagine,
to be headed here
all along. Stalled hour. Hour
of chronics. Never
is anything not done
less so. If you drink, by now
you might as well. If you cry,
by three your face
is salt. In grocery stores

you stare at cans. Studies
show your demographic
does well to take up
hobbies. Focus like a naturalist
on identifying varied calls
of band saws, jig saws,
skill saws. Or drowse
this heartland of the unemployed,
drawing evening like a blanket
from the east. It will quiet
soon, and night,
that good trick, is easier

than it looks. Moonlight maybes
up the streets. It's less difficult
to love what sleeps, because,

like you, it might wake up
new. Remembering
how bad luck flocks
is the slant of three. The hour
when you whisper
that used to be me,
while across municipalities
workers stride the day toward
the dinners they deserve.

Mirror

Evade your eye. Try to see as others do
what is desired or refused. What went wrong.
Or right, then wrong. Objectively, what hangs.
Pull yourself together. Years are neither kind
nor cruel. You drag on. The girl is gone.
Consider that it might be time to call in
a professional. Blood is fearless, runs
to meet a touch, indiscriminate, remembers
the first time it fell in love with the world, unaware
that now you are alone. Leave the bed,
the dress of sleep that so becomes you, buttoned
up with pills. You are simpler than you think,
your fading flush upon you as you stand,
only your constant name held in your hand.

Love Song of the Unreliable Narrator

Only God is objective, but he's long
gone, the thing that could save you
explained away. Irony takes you out at night
but appetite drives you home as I pace
outside your window singing songs
that make you moan with an uncertainty
that is the sex of dream. Lonely
as a preposition, you long for the thrust
of an accusative world. Crux. Locus.
Interstices. Can you feel my tug
upon your sleeve? The den that words
scratch out in you is my favorite haunt.
See my shadow; you'll have untold weeks
of whatever it is that you want.

Lucky

To be grateful is the condition
of strangers. For the suitcase of clothes
that fit. Stranger,

you have your favourite things
with you, and in pockets,
the ridiculous coloured bills

of your country. The waitress
who shows her fine wrists
to strangers is practical

as an integer, grace among
the overfed. You won't be remembered
leaving that Chevron, walking

flat-out into a brand new
minute. Be obliged
to this. Though you're without the sense

to give bad coffee a miss,
sugaring, milking, and it's clear
you don't learn. If you can name

one person who loves you among
all those for whom you are not quite
a stranger, try

to imagine yourself spoken of,
longed for. You may have to pull over
to the shoulder, even when

your own heart is gravel.
The rented room is clean. Touch
everything. No one

will knock. Stranger, you can do
what you want, prodigal, released
like an idea into the future. Without

policy, you take up very little
space. Your empathy, in the absence
of neighbours, astounding.

Emergency Response

You want love but not to give up anything
of your life, its situations –
whatever it is that you do. Never mind.
To hear this will bring no one any joy.
Something undoubtedly needs work. Surely
a knob has fallen off somewhere. The fixed
don't stay that way. It's a comfort,
actually, this perpetual loosening, the world
wearing on everything in it as when a taut hour
slackens into rain. Far greater for you
the consolation of repair, the glueing
and reglueing of various legs, all the snapped
handles. Raised by sandbaggers, you believe
in vise grips, in bolts. Now that what you want
has tooled in on its wobbly wheels
you've hauled up like a journeyman
with a wrench in your hand. And love
standing by, nearly in uniform, waiting
for it all to come apart.

AS IF

What, then, is contained in the *as if*? There must apparently
be something else hidden in it apart from the unreality and
impossibility of the assumption in the conditional sentence.
These particles clearly also imply a decision to maintain the
assumption *formally, in spite of* these difficulties. Between the
as and *if, wie* and *wenn, als* and *ob, comme* and *si, qua-si,* a
whole sentence lies implied.

— Hans Vaihinger

Found

Problems (A Meditation)

— From *Meteorology*. 6th ed. Richard A. Anthes. New Jersey: Macmillan, 1992.

How pure is the typical raindrop? Explain why there is some truth to the proverb "It's too cold to snow."

Is the dark side of the moon illuminated by earthlight as we are by moonlight?

Wind power has long been used to do a very minor portion of people's work. This is not too difficult to understand.

Is it practical?

What other factors, for example, characteristics of the wind, have not been considered?

In which sense does the vortex turn over your bathtub drain? Is the earth's rotation responsible? Would you expect any rotation if your bathtub were on the equator?

Consider the magnitude of forces.

Some proverbs state that physical appearances of certain insects and animals is an indication of future weather. Do you doubt their validity?

How would you classify the mean or standard lapse rate in the atmosphere as far as stability is concerned?

Why does smoke rise? Explain your answer.

Self-Portrait in a Series of Professional Evaluations

An excellent vocabulary, but spatial skills
are lacking. Poor in math. A bit uncoordinated,
possibly the inner ear? An eye exam
may be required. Not what you'd call a natural
athlete. Doesn't play well with others. Tries hard.

Fine sense of melody but a weak left hand. For God's sake
practice with a metronome. Your Chopin
is all over the place. Test scores indicate aptitude
for a career in the secretarial sciences. Handwriting
suggests some latent hostility. A diligent worker,
though often late. Please note:

an AC/DC t-shirt does not constitute professional
attire. You drove *how* long on the spare?
A good grasp of theory, though many sentence fragments
and an unusual fondness for semicolons; a tendency
toward unsubstantiated leaps. A black aura.

Needs to stroke essence of tangerine through the aura.
Should consider regular facials. Most people walk around
dehydrated all the time and don't even know it.
Normal. Negative. This month, avoid air travel
and dark-haired men. Focus on career goals.
Make a five-year plan.

Another Half-Hour Later in Newfoundland

Evening rises up. Hello. Apparently,
this thing still works. Old midway ride.
You've been on the shadow side
for hours watching crucial bolts fall off
and someone adrift at the switch.
How can we sleep through this? The creak
of struts that keep us equidistant
on the frame, from the hub, hot oiled
centre of the wheel, its eternal present
tense. Up top at noon you recognize
the common sense of parallel lines
as I harbour doubts about the inherent
strength of materials. Factoring in an act
of God, I miss the point completely.

Bomb Threat Checklist

> Open all windows in the immediate area.
> Evacuate the immediate area.
>
> — *University of Victoria Bomb Threat Checklist*

When will it blow? Where
is it now? What
does it look like? Do not trust your sense
of the ordinary. Anything you use
can turn against you:
a doorknob, a shoe, a telephone. Are you aware
of what could cause it to explode? Every day
we make our idle progress
among tripwire. You have no idea
of the pressure we're under.
Most of us: divorced.
All those little triggers.
Did you place the bomb? Why?
Why would you *do* that?
No insinuations have been made. We can help you
through this difficult time.
What is your address and your name? Your answers
may save your life.

We need the exact wording
of the threat. Leave it to us
to read between the lines. Language is a con. Please,
try to relax.
Peg the caller's age. What about sex? God knows
these days it's hard to tell.
We use the masculine pronoun for simplicity's sake.
How long was the call? You should've
kept him on the line. You really should be
more careful. Vigilance
is its own reward.

Where was it received? Date? Time?
You can tell your grandkids. Well,
you might.
Was there an accent? A dialect? Think.
We may have to worry
about everyone.

Consider the caller's state of mind. Was there laughter?
Tears? Some people meet their breaking point
softly, calmly, breathing
deep. Others clear their throats a lot. Keep in mind
that any voice can be disguised. Was it
deep? A ragged stutter?
Rapid? Nasal? Raspy? Slurred? Check all
that apply. Are drugs involved?
A sad childhood? Work
is a hotbed of discontent, as is thwarted, unprincipled,
worthless love.
You may well be our only hope.
Exciting, isn't it?
If the voice is familiar, who does it sound like?
This person may be known to us. This person
may be close to you.

The Vandal Confesses

Our hammers. Our sticks. This furtive
sporting life. Oh, our gasoline. Clothed
in low-rent autobiographies we slouch toward eviction
like dying brickworks. Outside

is day, a nice big one, floor upon floor
of well-mixed cocktails, and beyond the smog line,
a dissimulation of small birds. In darkness,
the city is a basement. We hunch in its hallways

like Goya's cats, low to the ground and brindled
with enigmatic rashes, stiff in the joints.
Glued together with rye, or blow, or glue,
we are a regular family.

*

Newspaper boxes, billboards, SUVs, Coke machines,
all is lost but for their breaking. We itch
and prosper heavenward on bands of grit and smoke,
our names, unknown, a bloody racket,

car alarm, nothing personal. We rip it up
alright. The trouble's not the tear-down,
it's the stall of afters when our hands hang.
The asking each to each what's next as we lean

inside like crummy tables. No wonder we don't feel
so well. Look here, soup is crawling
out of our bowls. The midtown Scotiabank's topmost
light has turned that cloud the colour of Cheezies.

*

There is a tenderness in things. In things,
ruined. As if, freed from functions we bend
them to, they are newborn to the prime
unalphabeted world. As though this were possible.

It doesn't matter. Burn it. Glass sparkles
my hair, my skin refined with ashes. I've pinched
what tools I own. *Material things,*
which have no soul, could not be true objects

for my love. Will I see you soon, candled
in the streetlit chalk of some immoderate place?
We could stand in wreckage and adored,
where nothing ever fades before it falls.

Parabola

Before words, mathematics nested in the Kananaskis
Valley, calculations of upsweep and plain an ache
in the bones of crow and Cooper's hawk. Hard

science lay fossilled in the scree: evolution,
cosine, fault. We camp by a river
full of fish. It's fall.

South, at Frank, the old town lies
in the cold arms of an equation. Mass,
velocity, a mountain broken by its weight. Path

of a projectile in the sway of gravity, Pythagorean music
as the rock came down. Those who remained built again,
just west, a place that rests like a miner on one knee

staring at the stripped logic of the northern slope
as engines throttle down and the sun, a plumb
bob, drops behind the seismic ridge.

Above our tent, leaves rattle dry
as fractals in the chill. His back
a warm and perfect arch.

Earlier, a young grizzly, collared,
tracked by men with dogs, humped
through campground cul-de-sacs, caught

in a tin net of dumpsters, shithouses, the racket
of trailers, wanting out to quick water and its autumn blooms
of cutthroat trout, the western crook of the valley where the berries

are good, too hungry yet for the high country, stumped by what's
bred in. Perhaps the first season alone. Yes, we wanted him
gone. Or at least far enough up on the rise, approximately

postcard size, a view: *Distant Landscape with Bear.*
Then to sleep, bodies sweet in careless symmetry
along the curve, congruent, unconcerned

by the prospect of an elemental grunt,
the indifferent variable rumbling in
to casually cancel us out.

The Problem of Heart Failure

> Murphy's Law is wrong – what *can* go wrong usually goes *right*. But
> then one day a few of the bad little choices come together …"
>
> — William Langewiesche

A cardiac concern in living colour on the laptop of a man
across the aisle, two rows up. I assume he's a doctor
though who isn't interested in the cranking
of that muscle? My own flimsy pump chugs on a slick
of Xanax, Jack chaser, a beer to smooth the pockets:
*Our superior fermentation technology now adds
more pleasure to your life.* Amen. Brothers, sisters,
what does it mean to prepare for cross-check? I'm iffy
and this the least of my worries 35,000 feet above
the Okanagan crater, tubed in steel propelled
by the most flammable substance on earth.
It's inconceivable, at 600 miles per hour, that people
will take off their shoes.

It's a kind of science, System Accident Thinking.
Mislabelled baggage. Wrench monkeys lurching through
mid-morning tequila flashbacks. The captain's
had a bitch of a day and the airstrip borders
a waterfowl preserve. Such inconsequentials converge
and a perfectly good aircraft nose dives
into Louisiana swampland, limbs scattered like receipts.
One whisky, one scotch, one beer. This is the problem
of heart failure: *the initiation and progression
of desire.* Pardon me. I've misread. That last word is
disease. Bad luck, bad habits. The unforeseen.
The doctor's screen shows a triangulation
of possibilities, the sanguine humour of geometry.

Found

Invariants

From *Analytic Geometry*. 2nd ed. R.S. Underwood and
Fred. W. Sparks. Cambridge: The Riverside Press, 1956.

The answer consists of equations replaced by the values
found above. Here we stop, noting that we have done
all that was required in the problem. Note that the work
of carrying through substitutions would be tedious
in this case, and that therefore other methods
of dealing with equations of this type should be sought.

Describe the family of curves. Find the common eccentricity,
when the loci exist. Describe the family and find
the common eccentricity. Describe the family.
Show that the members of the family are pairs
of parallel lines. Show that a term cannot be introduced
into the equation by rotation of axes.

Science and the Single Girl

Initially, an unbecoming enthusiasm
for dissection. What's dead
is dead and some unborn
will stay that way. All things find purpose
in the end, even the done-for,
done-in. But when it flinched
at the pin, she dumped the earthworm out the window
to the lawns and fled. Spring robins
waddling in the grass she narrow-eyed
with a resurrected Catholic dread
that longs to love the world
for what it gives, but sees the glint
of sacrifice in everything that lives.

x is all that is denied. Not erased,
per se, for a twitchy something lies
beneath those crossbeams for which *x*s on the eyes
stand in. *y* isn't finished with this yet.
It's the question of intent. In formula
they are pregnant, chromosomal
with design, with what waits
to be realized as correct and absolute. The truth
beyond the equal sign.

All things being equal, they are not.
What can we expect of a triangle
that we cannot expect from ourselves? Each side
a retaining wall, holding up its end. But
an equilateral affair? Please. At most,
scalene – the short straw, long
edge, and what bears up in between. The law.
Rhombus means watch out: your house
is falling down around your ears.
Look at them, drawn. Nothing gets out
or in. Perimeters secure and air inside the smell
of zero. A circle is never getting clear
of the woods, finding only the body, again and again
a leaky approximate. Despite theologies
of equation, the protractor's gleam
and grin, it's impossible to square all angles
fair. The arc can't straighten up its game,
bails out on the curve,
while congruency rides its dreary rails
like an accident waiting to begin.

Parallel to the sensible horizon bounding
the observer's view, where earth or sea
and sky appear to meet, there is one called rational,
or true. A matter of belief in what does not
reveal itself. Brief measure of comfort, then a moment
of iceblink: *white glare on the underside*
of a distant cloud caused by reflection
from a mass of ice which may itself be too far away
to be visible. It reminds you of a man you barely know,
the discordant coast of his Atlantic
irregularities. Begin to read in topographical maps
the physical relief of him. Salinity and scar.
Rock-glacier: *a tongue or stream*
which moves gradually downwards through the action
of alternate frost and thaw. A blind valley
is *where the stream disappears underground.*
Brave west winds storm with regularity and force
while from watershed flows the variable course
of his heart. Between Capricorn and Cancer
lies the Torrid Zone, wrung and wet, never oblique
in its fevers; but nearby, the high-pressure belt
of Horse Latitudes' horrid dead-eye calms. Either way,
a long, mean solar day. *Solution is one form*
of weathering. A loss of headwaters at the elbow
of capture. Winds of atmospheric depression.
Sensual agencies wearing away the geography
that keeps you apart or together. Anticline: *see Syncline.*
Mouth: *see River.*

Chance

Theory grins like a rat and won't flip. Gives up only that nothing
is forbidden: time backpedalling toward the great divide
and air haywiring out of the room
altogether, weird as a cat. Whatever.

I've seen stranger. Odds
piled up and smug that way, then the World Series,
1951. Then any seventh game. Origins of flight. Or the nail
that keeps your foot in mind. *Why*

is a coy dead end. Shine your beam
in its eyes, shove it against the wall. Laws clam up like henchmen,
twitchy and forlorn, rapt to the criminal potential of perpetual
motion. So these things don't occur

in the goddamned observable world. Not yet.
Screw precedent. Give me a phone book and five minutes alone.
Bring coffee. Bring
something. It's a life's work.

Probability is all we're left, hazard and gamble
our most rational precincts. Should we crack this one, the future
would open like a late-game lead. And we could use it.
Boy could we.

Determinism

Someone's walking toward you, tree to tree, parting leaves
with the barrel of a rifle. There's a scope
on it. He's been watching awhile
through his good eye, you, washing dishes, scouring
what's burned with a handful of salt, so your shoulders shake
a little. Keep your back to him. It's sexier
under the bulb, light degraded,
like powder. The kitchen screens
are torn. You've worn something
nice. There's a breeze he's pressing through, boots
in the grass. There's a breeze and you smell him
blowing in on it. As if this has always
been happening and you've entered the coincidence of your life
with itself, the way a clock's ticks will hit the beat of a Hank Williams song,
the best one, on the radio, fridge hum tuned without a quaver
to the sustained notes of the bridge. As if
you've arrived at where the hinge
articulates. An animal
may be bleeding in the woods. He could be carrying a pair of grouse
by the feet. Only details are left, bruises of gesture, style's aspirin
grit. He shuts the door and leans the gun against the wall
like a guitar. You keep your back to him because
it's sexier. Because in turning
you will see the dinner in all its potential
as you speak, spring the catch, finish this, the weighted moment
buckling into consequence. The place
where you can face your history and see it coming.

Your Premiums Will Never Increase

> Accidents can include permanent attributes of a thing; the
> technical meaning of the term is very broad.
>
> — Glossary. *Hellenistic Philosophy: Introductory Readings.*

As if it couldn't wait. One would've kept driving
but for a wrecked air conditioner and record
high temperatures in the parkland. Who, cut off
at a blind approach and had it, cranked the wheel
toward a tourist trap to see a friend. The other,
in this company, was bold. They met by accident,

which is normal. That spring, a bear airlifted
miles from the townsite to a wilderness section
of the protected zone was back in four days. Warnings
were posted and generally ignored. Through
the summer they wrote each other on the loveliness
of this and that, in the inevitable dialect, and surprised

themselves in bed. During a rare electrical storm
over Vancouver Island, a giant sequoia was split dead
centre. One half fell on a citizen's Saab, the other half
on his house. *What are the chances?* he laughed,
well-insured, to the press. Elsewhere, people won
prizes. Several more gave up. Others kept driving.

There are two kinds of motion, the straight
and the swerve. By winter, what passed between them
had done so, leaving evidence of the glitch winking
glib as a stripped screw. Sure, here was the trouble
all along. Some things don't turn out for the best,
and are not even interesting. Forget them. Because
this is about you, and what happens next.

Meeting Walter Benjamin

A long lake in a swan-throated bed, longer
than wide by seventy miles. In his loneliness you mistake him
for shade creaking from the poplars, his gait that way,
eyes down, backlit, its yet-againness. He mistakes you in kind
for a snag of brome, for in your loneliness
you have forgotten the grammar of description – no,
the *why* of it – and become just another little bit
of what's there, unable as grass is to explain itself. Here,
above the mudline of a Saskatchewan valley, and he
has never seen one. When he speaks
it's from midpoint over the dog-hued water, his voice
thrown, a bond loosened and winging on the updraft
past your ear. It's real, he says,
your disappointment. Wind stirs up hill colour like a stick
in paint, Fauvist with hidden deer in this seed-heavy
fall among a wet year's curious late-bloomers, the air convex,
retinal. Follow his eye: *Angelus Novus* up against
the barbed wire, blown backward, disconsolate as anyone
with a grasp of history. You've read that grace
abides in a law of downward motion. He says despair
is in the details. Don't look,
he tells you. Then, look.

Sleeping with Wittgenstein

Not everything you look at
is something. What was true is

no longer, and belief
a problem of tenses, of lapse. It's like this,

he says. The sad are charmless.
When I broke the treeline, found

the shore, he was halfway
across. I balked. Certain prospects

appear deeper than they are or flatten
on the shoals of aspect-

blindness: an inability to see
the double cross. I'm drenched. He's a man

who gets over it. Onward and steeled,
a compass. Without him,

I might have died in those woods. I say,
Hit it with a hammer. Sometimes

that works. I say Listen,
I'm alone here. Now he's speculating

if it's possible to control
the electrics with a panel of small

levers, from bed. The window, fixed
expertly, opens again. Next to it

I'm imperfectly dried, ears back, ungratefully
putting two and two together.

Found

Elementary Calculus

From *Elementary Calculus*. A. Keith and W. J. Donaldson.
Glasgow: Gibson, 1960.

Speed (like distance)
is a magnitude and has no
direction; velocity (like displacement)

has magnitude and direction.
Thus we may say
that after 4 seconds

the stone is travelling at a speed
of 32 feet per second,
but if we wish to remove all doubts

as to the direction of motion
we must add the word
downwards.

Returning to the problem
about the stone
we have sometimes written

32 ft. per (sec.)^2. The reader
should think out for himself
why the phrase *per second*

occurs twice. The quantity
in question sounds more meaningful
if read: *32 feet per second*

– pause –

per second.

Cipher Stroke

> Scores of cases of the 'stroke' are reported among men and women of all classes, who have been prostrated by their efforts to figure in thousands of millions. Many of these persons apparently are normal, except for a desire to write endless rows of ciphers.
>
> — John Kenneth Galbraith

India opened zero and gods crawled out. Then everything else
fell in. Became, in falling, infinitely lovely, lit
with presence. Light in the still-life, spark in the field
we angle toward, odd-numbered
in a wonky sorrow, sight-lined to the vanishing point
with no end to speak of. Backs up against it,
the Greeks stared at stars for a long time, whistling,
beginning at one: the Prime Mover, itself
unmoved, blameless in a fast fade.

~

It has the tug of a hole about it,
that hole, the mortal instant that fevers, shines,
then resumes its mileage hill to hill. A hundred kilometres
between Seven Persons and Purple Springs means
an easy hour on the highway. Unless the traffic's
bad, or the weather's bad, or the engine's bad, or worse
should an alarming new equation involving plastics
and combustion be borne in on the shoulders
of a huge misunderstanding. Please
tell me to shut up over and over. You drive.
I can't keep my eyes open.

~

Careers are made of it. To be proven wrong
and to try to make even this
beautiful. Find us in the fields again, the bush,
or back in the slapworn towns we grew up in, counting
off. As if we could forward or reverse along
the path of weird degrees and close the distance separating
us from what we love. The in-between
exponentiates merrily as a debt. And then, and
then. Repeat yourself and see what happens.

~

It's said the stock market behaves organically,
like a rodent or a wave. Everyone has a system
to own the table. Odds are night will fall
unnoticed, with the tick of water wasting through a hose
as the house burns down. Can thought about things
be so much different from things? Take up sleep
and defensive drinking. Lie down
awhile. At the airport, planes take off
and land without a problem.

~

Nothing keeps happening. A special kind
that pulls our midpoints toward it. The lure of the lip
where the falling starts, hesitant apex
of the arc or the prairie exhaling through centuries,
its great unseen beams sistered up, looking like the convergence
of an infinite series where each instant, each sound
hides another, and so on. Silence, the breath
inside the body of what is, sings an unbroken tone struck
in the key of nil. This endless untitled exclamation
implicit and from everywhere at once.

EVERYTHING'S OKAY

Found

Publications in Natural History

— *A Bibliography.* British Columbia Provincial Museum, 1971.

Amphibians of British Columbia. The Reptiles
of British Columbia. Fresh Water Fishes. Birds:
Woodpeckers.

Crows and Their Allies.

Barnacles. Shorebirds. The Grasses. Upland
Game Birds of British Columbia. The Mammals.

Ferns and Fern-allies of British Columbia. Birds:
Gulls.

Alien Animals in British Columbia.

Waterfowl. Orchids. Intertidal Bivalves. The Birds
of British Columbia: Owls. The Heather Family
(*Ericaceae*). A Guide to Common Edible Plants.

A Guide to Marine Life. Birds:
Chickadees, Thrushes, Kinglets, Waxwings, Pipits,
and Shrikes.

Common Marine Fishes of British Columbia. A Guide
to Mushrooms.

The Lily Family of British Columbia.
Seaweeds. Some Mosses.

More Intertidal Bivalves.

Birds: Divers and Tube-nosed Swimmers.
The Rose Family.

An Occasional Paper Series. Out of Print.
The Mosquitoes of British Columbia. Please
send cheque or money order, payable:

The Minister of Finance of British Columbia.

Under the Sun

Rain is the merging of cool air with warm
under general conditions of humidity. Try to remember
it has nothing to do with love
or grief. This is the consolation of philosophy:
it's out of our hands. The business of bars
and stores, our separate beds, the garbaged
offices of alleyways, is aging. It sighs
in the blood like salt, slows us, and is why
our hearts are heaviest on the moment
of waking: the weight we ferry, the fright,
the long vowel opening at the centre
of a consonant world that draws the hurt up,
an empty bowl, while history's rebar is replaced
and a species coughs its lungs out
in another room. Private lives of insects
and the single notes that move them, hard-won
courage of raccoon and crow who eat our garbage
and hate us, are foreclosed. We are lonely. We
are here. Inside, a vestigial swimmer bears
memory like a phantom pain of when the earth
was new and we were a promise in the sex
of its making, its heat and pools. Cells' random
liquid birth. In the molecular ache of land
as it cooled, when, before tears, before
property, it rained for more than a million years.

Thanksgiving

On an afternoon so still it's possible to see
how the world can fill the holes we make
and complete itself again. Or how desperately
we want this to be so. Downstream,
Dad hauled an 18-pound pike into the boat
and we saw no change in the river.
Water closed as its tail left the surface,
continued to reflect for us what we needed
from clear sky, wild poplar, red maple,
from the last warm day of that year.

Near Bull's Head, mule deer wander the streets
of Estuary, a village abandoned when CN tore out
its only bridge for miles. That they feed
on wild onion and millet, from gardens flung
to seed, looked fine to us, if not holy,
though we knew people who had lived there,
who cried moving their beds from the valley.
Even Hutterite cattle blunting through wolf willow,
sweet sage ghosting around them,
seemed closer to the animal they once were.

We drove away at twilight, the fish curled
in a blue plastic basin, gills reaching for the place
that had so plainly surrendered it. Our heads
were full of how seldom we are together now,
and when my mother prepared the flesh
my father had provided, we took into ourselves
its longing to be home.

The Bench

It's noon, hot, and you're wondering how you hoped
to find peace in a place that doesn't want you.
Decades ago, camping here with family, sweetgrass
and the book of stars seemed a gracious guide
to being in the world. Now you are merely something
for deer to avoid, and all you love
even less than that. Skulls of badger, red fox,
elk's long bones, bleach and settle in the way
things drained of instinct become a kind of stone. Land
neither remembers nor forgets. Battle Creek,
once red with blood, is clear again. Ice that carved
an ancient seabed north of Maple Creek
cracked on these granite hills, split east and west
to converge again southbound into Montana. This history
concerns you less than the accident of birth
that brought you here, local, to the borderland
between provincial parks. The girl you were found respite
from unending wheatfields in its meals of trout
and blessed shade, and you moved away imagining
a blue tent pitched forever by the lake. Mosquitoes
rise in tune from its muddy shore. Animals
light the evening lamps of their eyes and wait for you
to leave, for the city to reclaim you. Where
your new car fits the avenues precisely.

Montana

To a stranger, the word is open. Vowels a body
could fall through, loose-shouldered as a cat
onto a bed of sweetgrass, looking up
from the great plain. Prayers for rain and an end
to winter have filled the sky with stars.
That they are empty of the matter that made them,
light without heat, is unimportant,
for we are used to making beautiful those deaths
that are not ours. Hugo's ghost
bounces like a steelhead off Missoula's pleasant walls.
He's gone underground, head beneath a rock
somewhere. We drink ourselves to tears
in the Milltown Union Bar.

There's shopping to do: cheap Marlboros
and whiskey. Helena, pretty daughter, presses up
against the Lewis Range. Babb goes crazy
in its northern cage in the cursed way
of border towns, while east, on the flatland,
Havre bangs in the wind. Open liquor.
Open road. The bars do well, blinking sleepless
in the scrub. Old ranchers cough bad weather
from their lungs, killing time.
Dead wives ghost the gravel roads.

On loan to ourselves, we are breathless
with holiday, backlit by gilt grasslands
of the Blackfoot nation, each afternoon
an embarrassment of riches. In Butte and Billings,
bored farm boys and edgy barmaids stalk
side streets after hours, their lives in shifts.

Corporate agriculture, franchise, and celebrity retreats
spread like cream across the counties. We turn
north to the border, duty-free waiting.
A firm handshake. Our civil right. Souvenirs
of the places we visit, by which we are
so seldom changed.

Lines Composed a Few Miles above Duncairn Dam

The reservoir is fed by Swift Current Creek. It's small,
a half mile by six, and has the itch going for it. Snail flukes
can't feed on people but they try. The fishing's good.
It's stocked.

On the north side, squatters' cabins and planted
shade trees. Further up is the dump. Burn pit, fish guts,
trash. Recall the neighbours. You can't just do
whatever you want. There are certain kinds
of boating. Gull Lake's close. We all drive.

On the south side are bluffs, and cows meant
for beef. There are dens in the few wild groves. Muskrats
like thin old men who've made machine shops
of their living rooms. Coyotes too. It's not a great idea
to keep chickens.

There's a rumour. A pipeline leak below the lakebed
and natural gas bubbles the size of apricots popping
at the surface. This may or may not be true,
as usual.

Simmie, adjacent, was a town once. The little plank church
makes a good photograph. Someone's junk is in it.

The store, next to the beverage room, sells smokes
and low-end booze, rat traps, potato wedges, shampoo,
Raid, ice cream, cribbage boards, Crazy Glue,
buffalo wings, rubber gloves, line and lures,

etc. Leeches can be purchased from the pop machine
outside, a half-dozen for $1.25. A sweet life:
Coke, Seven-Up, water, bait. You could walk from the lake
but no one does.

To follow a sightline over the fields is a long, long
look. Wind has a good time there. Your eye
will tear over and close.

I write this on a plane, two days before
the 100th anniversary of flight, 37,000 feet above
Lake Ontario. Above the cloud above Lake Ontario.

Gopher

Dirt divers, you pop up, fast and fleshy weeds. We turn
our ankles where you've been and bust your heads
for fun. In the lab of summertime we experiment the finer points
of poison, snares, gasoline, twist your tails off at the root,
then finally, old enough, use that Christmas .22 gifted
lovingly, oiled, with a big red bow. You eat and breed. We try
to drown you out. You're thieves, and we can't spare a thing.
In winter, as you coma deep inside your rancid holes,
we satisfy ourselves chasing rabbits with Ski-doos
until spring when hungry coyotes raid the coops and we need
to shoot them too. They kill the fawns, reserved
for city hunters who pay cash to anyone who'll take them
through the fields. Each season has its cruelties. It's for the best.
Is nature not more callous than the gun? First and precious
taste of blood, there's always more where you come from.

Pest Song

Your habits drew me. I could tell by the way
you leave the milk out at night, bread box open
and grains untied, that you are passionate
and I was smitten, lived with you for months

before you knew I was alive, learned the wiring
of your moods, drinking from your cups
and tasting leaves of every book you've read, sly
and devoted as a friend. Forgetting the wisdom

of my kind, I cried out one night when you walked
through the door, and the set of your mouth
was a new kind of poison. You say
there can never be just one. It's understood.

But be assured, you don't know everything. I am
alone. When you bring others to our home
I make a scene. If they really loved you, they
would stay. I rest on your pillow, lick your soap,

embrace your toothbrush while you're gone. Now
you're setting traps, eyes mean as bleach,
but I can't believe you really want to do me harm.
You'd miss me and not know why, my voice,

the grace notes of my feet. So I keep my hunger
wrapped up tight, watch my step, come out late
to stare at you from some dark place, and wait
until you're fast asleep before kissing you goodnight.

Found

The Birds of British Columbia

— From *The Birds of British Columbia: (4) Upland Game Birds.*
Victoria: British Columbia Provincial Museum, 1971.

In no other game bird but the ruffled grouse do the tones
of gray, black, cinnamon and white shade and blend
with such quiet harmony. Child of the wilderness
that he is, in the full dark pupil of that eye surrounded
by an iris of October's own brown, seem always to dwell
the brooding shadows of the great forest he loves
so well. And in the moulding of him Nature seems
to have embodied all the beauty, all the charm, all
the inexplicable strangeness and romance of the autumnal
woods and produced her feathered masterpiece. Always
is he the woodland's pride, alert, instinct with life, and filled
with a spirit and a dash that furnishes, in such mixed cover
as we were hunting this day, the very climax
of shooting with the shotgun.

Thrasher

Yellow-legs ekes lower at nightfall to a stick nest
brambled in the shade-kill, doing for himself, deft

as a badger in a hammock. Mornings, toeing wracked heights
of the cottonwood, he flaps his brown flag above alkaline

slough beds, over plowlands attesting
to the back and forth of work, their brown degrees

scriven by road allowance cut at right angles through shriven
weeds, fenceposts bracketing brown rut lines slantwise

in relief. In relief at the topmost, he mimics domestic, migrant,
spaniel, spring peepers, quacks, urks, and gurgles akin

to a four-stroke in heavy water. He's slightly

off. None respond. His own call is the vinyl scratch
between tracks, a splice point. He was hatched

that way, ferruginous, a wet transistor
clacking from the egg in which he had lain curled

as an ear with an itch inside. He carries on
like AM radio. Like a prison rodeo. Recounts loser

baseball teams, jerry-riggers, part-timers, those paid in scrip,
anyone who has come out of retirement once

too often. He is playbacks, do-overs, repeats, repeats
the world's clamorous list, makes it his, replete,

and fledges from persistence what he is.

Parallax

Two white rabbits on an autumn fallow field
seem an argument for jumping the snowfall.
For readyness bred in. A fur that knows from birth
what's best if you are prey. Keep still. But wait,
that's wrong. They stick out like dumplings in a stew
for coyote, hawk, and gun. They've rushed their cue.
For them, the season may be botched. I walk on,
eyes to the ground. It's how I think.

Through the wiffle and purr of gas wells that pock
the Wilde Hills, a far-off crang of men
unloading pipe. Roads are creased with ruts
their trucks make. We own no mineral rights.
Companies pay rent for land surveyed, dug up
and drilled. The money helps. Around sites, at angles,
we plant wheat under sky we're known for,
the gradient amount of it, enjoy down times at night
around the fire pit raising whisky to the health
of weather and machines. On our own place
we burn what we like. Underground is water we don't
drink. It's been no good for years.

Seventy-five years past the town went dry. No rain,
no booze. A few parched men half on a lark, half
nuts with thirst, rolled the tavern shack onto a flat,
hauled it past the limits of the law. Drank bootleg
until told to bring it back. And did. And the dust
flew in gusts and swells. Tons hovered in the odd
calm. Lard rasped. Linens scratched. Horses died.
But this is all written in books, and taken care of.

A partridge flushed from ditch weed beats away,
a fat pulse racing through morning air warmish

and skunky with additives. I look up and squinting
see that what I took for rabbits are in fact
two empty plastic herbicide containers –
perhaps Horizon or Refine – blown from a half-ton bed
and half sunk in dirt. I curse Monsanto and the rest,
my nearsighted eyes. Inherited, bad on both sides.

The government once saw fit to give this land away,
there being only grass and Indians on it. Stones
from teepee rings host lichen in the rockpiles
as corporations draw a bead on the flyover zone
posing buy-outs like questions to those for whom
there are none. It's hard, when things get worse
for years. Fall carries on as usual. Cranes gurgle
in the stubble. Repairs are made. We go fishing.

It's the animal season. Even for those hunted
the tin smell of incipient frost means an itch for food
and a specific hidden bed. Something troubles stems
at the culvert mouth ahead, where grid and road
allowance meet, something skinking through foxtails
with alpha nose or acute eye that knows this place
as it is. There are no themes. Just this creature only what
it is, whatever that may be. I can't tell from here.

Pastoral

I hold a short softwood stick some worm took to
and runnelled with its mouth parts, ambling
as it ate. Note how its carvings imitate
furlings of the mildly impressive waterfall
still at it, chewing the valley. And these again
in whorls of amber gunk oozing from a pine.
Worm-addled stick, river, sap, my fingerprints, all of it
points in patterns on a complex plane: A Julia
Set. We even sound the same, a surge of air
and fluids, though I beaver myself up
with cigarettes and booze and jut from the cliffside
like a mine disaster. You should see what I cough
from my lungs at night. Gasses and dust
of one stupid thing after another. I'm here to relax

even as noxious weeds overrun the parkland:
mugwort, foxtail, stinkweed, goatsbeard, dropped
from hindquarters of foreign Airstreams jackknifing
in the townsite. I look for beauty and find it,
floored by lichen's radial grace and the incisive liquor
of juniper. Upending rocks, parting creeping spruce,
I exclaim each time: *Aha!*
An indigenous squirrel regards me squarely
from a branch. Cougars are culling local pets,
elk calve with murder in their eyes, and it's the worst
tick season in 40 years. The whole valley
is out for blood, for itself. As, of course, am I.

An Argument for Small Arms

The shock is that it took
so long, this trajectory played out
in a fizzle toward the words
I understand. By suppertime
on the first day of what's left, the stock
of a small bore .22 fits smartly
at the shoulder. Home,
home. Suppose this is it. Loaded.
Levelled. A rote stance
squared off to the fence
and the trash set up there. Empties.
Their cylindrical shadows lie
uneasily upon the ragweed. This
is the man-made moment. Extension
of the arm, the eye, the mind's
follow-through to an end
in shards. The clap and recoil
of continuity cracked. Air torn
like a letter through the middle
of before and after.

English Bay

The captain's come ashore and vanished
in the city's downtown east end. The bad side. He's likely involved
in a vagrancy. The crew waits and waits

then radios in. It's Vietnamese, mostly,
and the freighter licensed to a corporate office in Brunei
where a telephone on the floor rings on and on.
Hold full of bolts and washers tooled specifically,
it bobs dispiritedly as Pluto. Socklike,
the flag of origin hangs.

The men are denied leave to land. It's feared they will disappear
through countless doors of the regional district
and further burden its social systems. Provisions boated out
by charitable agencies are received in tightening
silence. As though a skin were forming.

Because the men are growing liverish
and stiffening. Threats of pirates, storms, failures
of structural integrity, now this.

Bilge water swells and rot proceeds on schedule.
Time is welding the men to the ship's body parts.
Their pipes knock. In bunks below the waterline
they hear the rusty gut of the Pacific creaking on its hinge,
feel its bile pressing,

and on fine days stand on deck looking inland
to where residents in street clothes walk small dogs forever
along the sea wall.

The Apartments

When I sleep it's on the 11th of 12 floors. Where I lie
and think *a thing tends downward*, then get up
and pace my way into an actual condition. The carpet
is maroon. A forensic opportunity.
I've seen this from sidewalks: curtains
water stained, cigarette burnt, flapping sallow
through a screenless open window, and wondered
at such rooms and what goes on. Now I know.
It's not much.

. . . .

In 1790, Xavier de Maistre toured his flat and composed
a travelogue: *Journey Around My Bedroom.* Eight years later
he set off again, by night this time,
to the window ledge, and wrote *Nocturnal Expedition
around My Bedroom.* By thirty-five
there was no reason to believe his life
was elsewhere.

. . . .

A little patience, some legwork, and it could have turned out
differently. Without elevators, their shafts,
and messages coughed out in puffs of cleaning fluid smell.
Fake pine with something else underneath. It's mid-October,
and rig crews have headed up to Fort McMurray.
There again: that thump in the hall, dry creak, then a sound
like a sack of historical novels whumping
down the lurid documentary of the garbage chute.
I can only guess. Someone smokes in bed. Someone's
left the stove on.

. . . .

All men naturally hate each other, explains Pascal,
a hypochondriac. As was Glenn Gould,
who was right.

. . . .

But what a view! Sun small for its age hand-over-handing
to a shaky hang above the refinery as leaves let go
along the North Saskatchewan in a failure of nerve
at the early frost. Persons
walk raised glass pedways between malls, unaware
of the covert habits of architects. Traffic
is a deal struck downtown. On this strip,
most single family homes have been condemned. It's possible
to imagine those abandoned leaning to the valley's song
of wood and dirt, if one cared to.
They'll be replaced by condominiums which,
like certain breeds of ornamental dog, do not
age well. Weak jointed, they're a make-work
project. Few taxpayers stroll the streets, unable to find
one good reason.

. . . .

Preserving farness, nearness presences nearness in nearing
that farness. Bringing near in this way, nearness conceals itself
and remains, in its way, nearest of all. This is very clearly
Heidegger. He saw it, the plainness at dusk
as objects turn inward and give us
their surfaces. The river's thickset light
is not its own.

. . . .

Across the street, a bulb burns on in a vacant penthouse suite
forgotten by a realtor with a roast in the oven. White cupboards,
white walls, a long black hall. I stare from my couch,
full of plots, fearing I am not a credible witness
to the red right hand of any crime
that might take place on my watch. Perhaps
it will be me, or reasonable facsimile, holding up a paper
upon which something, presumably,
is written.

. . . .

Simone Weil asks of solitude, *Where does its value lie?*
It filled her up like rain until, the way a gauge is,
she was emptied.

. . . .

Today an early snow against which those who should know better
spin their wheels. At the expensive hour of evening
when lamps come on, some tenants carry bags
up from below. For others
who stay in all day, dinners planned since noon are now spots
and crumbs. On the eighth floor an old man lives
with his Boston Terrier. *She is my world,*
he says. Looks me in the eye and tells me that.
Linda, on four, advises regulars in the bar downstairs
she loves them. *But hell,*
I love everybody. Meanwhile, outside the city,
a missing child who toddled the trajectory of his new eye
into the hills is found alive, under a tree. Possibly
we have never been happier.

. . . .

All dwellings have something of the grave about them, writes
Jean Baudrillard. Whom I've never particularly liked.

Seven Days

I

On the threshold of a room by the week.
Motel at the fringe of the Greater Municipal Area,
lakeside. From here it looks alright, the city,
and its major structures solid and unpeopled.
Like outcrops, they have simply occurred.
Small craft potter to and fro among the islands.

II

An exercise in looking on the move.
Between home and gone when the two won't separate,
like modern milk. The sound of traffic
is without address. One might think of air
bending on the non-Euclidian plane.

III

To be a little bored. A little.
To sit upon a span of lawn and ride the day out.
But the world has bats in it, these remarkable
trees – what are they? –
and people drive by in cars. Cars!

IV

Whatever the thing, heart or mind, it is easily
made glad when unobserved. Purple martins
do their feeding on the fly as two German chambermaids

next door repeat a word. Elsewhere
advancements are being made. The yacht club
offers free boat rides.

V

It is nominally summer and moreover nearly evening.
All particles possess a wavelike aspect.
Lights of the skyline are now becoming visible
the way stars would. Of stars,
nothing can be said.

VI

Against the city so anxiously made up,
swans seem a deliberate act. Best to be in love
as is the gauge with what it measures:
shaken, flooded, blown, then left alone.

VII

A final afternoon opens.
The lake, a great wing, rises to it.

Everything's Okay

And the sun with spin on it now, with hover. Lower over
the light industrial west end, shot back by windowed towers
of the Big Three, it blinds you coming

and going, something smart with your name on it. Spring
walks all over us on sharp heels. Spring chants its way
through the playoffs. Things, being things,

have never been better. Here on the grid, you have reason
to appreciate urban planning more than anything
your parents ever taught you, as Lake Ontario sleeps

with its freighted eye open under sky like a smoker's
bedclothes. Say *Igreja Universal do Reino de Deus*
until you mean it, say Roncesvalles until you buy that bit

about beauty in ugliness, under oath as you are to living
for the moment, uncut, blow by blow. A woman sings
karaoke in a third floor flat, while below an engine grinds,

trying to turn over. Behind café glass, a man leans
to his companion as though he loves her. You believe one idea,
and then another. That is, in the instant, at the time.

Notes on the poems

The entry for "dwell" is from *Klein's Comprehensive Etymological Dictionary of the English Language*. Ed. Dr. Ernest Klein. Unabridged 1 vol. 8th ed. Amsterdam: Elsevier, 2003.

The Diane Arbus quote used as an epigraph to "Nice" is from tape recordings of a series of classes she gave in New York City in 1971, some of which are transcribed in *Diane Arbus: An Aperture Monograph*. (Ed. Doon Arbus and Marvin Israel. New York: MOMA, 1972).

The passage by Hans Vaihinger introducing the second section is from *The Philosophy of 'As If'* (Trans. C.K. Ogden. 6th ed. London: Routledge, 1965).

"Bomb Threat Checklist" contains a number of lines taken directly from the *Bomb Threat Checklist* distributed to offices at the University of Victoria.

The italicized lines on the second page of "The Vandal Confesses" are from Saint Augustine's *Confessions* (Trans. R.S. Pine-Coffin. London: Penguin, 1976).

William Langewiesche's "The Lessons of Valujet 592," quoted as an epigraph to "The Problem of Heart Failure," was published in *The Atlantic Monthly* (March, 1998) pp. 81-98. The first italicized lines in that poem appear on cans of Pacific Dry Beer, served for a time on Air Canada flights originating in British Columbia. No kidding.

The italicized lines in the fourth section of "Science and the Single Girl" are definitions included in *The Penguin Dictionary of Geography* (Ed. W.G. Moore. 6th ed. London: Penguin, 1981).

The epigraph to "Your Premiums Will Never Increase" was taken from *Hellenistic Philosophy: Introductory Readings* (Trans. Brad Inwood and L.P. Gerson. Indianapolis: Hackett Publishing Company, Inc., 1988). The first sentence of the last stanza is Epicurus as noted by Aetius and appears also in this volume.

The *Angelus Novus* referred to in "Meeting Walter Benjamin" is a Paul Klee painting acquired by Benjamin in 1921. Of it, he wrote: "This is how one pictures the angel of history. His face is turned toward the past. Where we perceive a chain of events, he sees one single catastrophe which keeps piling wreckage upon wreckage and hurls it in front of his feet. The angel would like to stay, awaken the dead, and make whole what has been smashed. But a storm is blowing in from Paradise; it has got caught in his wings with such violence that the angel can no longer close them. The storm irresistibly propels him into the future to which his back is turned, while the pile of debris before him grows skyward. This storm is what we call progress." (*Illuminations*. Trans. Harry Zohn. New York, 1968.)

The first line of "Sleeping with Wittgenstein," as well as a discussion of "aspect-blindness," are included in Wittgenstein's *Philosophical Investigations* (Trans. G.E.M. Anscombe. New York: Macmillan, 1953).

The epigraph to "Cipher Stroke" is from John Kenneth Galbraith's *Money: Whence it Came, Where it Went.* (London: A. Deutsch, 1975).

The advertisement supplying the epigraph to "The Apartments" appeared in the December, 2004 issue of *Harper's Magazine.* Subsequent references in that poem are as follows:

Xavier de Maistre wrote *Voyage autour de ma Chambre* while confined to quarters following a duel in the winter of 1790. It was published in Turin in 1794. The *Expédition nocturne autour de ma Chambre* was published in Paris by Dondey-Dupré in 1825. Though it was actually written between 1799 and 1823 during his time in Russia serving in the czar's army, the attic room he describes is the one he occupied in Turin. And as before, there are allusions to real persons and events.

Blaise Pascal's explanation is from *Pensées* (Trans. A.J. Krailsheimer. London: Penguin, 1966).

The Martin Heidegger lines appear in *Poetry, Language, Thought*. (Trans. Albert Hofstadter. New York: Harper & Row, 1971).

Simone Weil asks this in *Gravity and Grace*. (Trans. Emma Craufurd. London: Routledge, 1987).

This observation by Jean Baudrillard is one of a great many included in *America*. (Trans. Chris Turner. London: Verso, 1988).

References for the found poems throughout the book appear below their titles. Except for line breaks, the original text of these pieces is unaltered.

Acknowledgments

Some of these poems have appeared, in earlier versions, in *CV2, Descant, Grain, Other Voices, Maisonneauve, Prairie Fire, The Fiddlehead, The Malahat Review, This Magazine, Vallum,* in the anthology *Open Field: 30 Contemporary Canadian Poets* (New York: Persea, 2005), and in the chapbook *The Shooter's Bible* (Junction Books, 2004). My appreciation to the editors of each.

The Canada Council for the Arts, Ontario Arts Council, and Toronto Arts Council provided financial support that allowed completion of this book. I extend special thanks to the Banff Centre for the Arts and the University of Alberta English Department.

I'm indebted once again to my editor, Barry Dempster, for his patience and skill in guiding the surgeries. Cheers also to Carleton Wilson, the brain, brawn, and heart of Junction Books.

To my bandmates: Kimberley Peter, Käri Sackney and Janet Walters. And to Gus Butterfield, Ford Pier, and John Sauvé for listening and all that it entails. I'm grateful to Ken Babstock and David Seymour for assistance editorial and otherwise.

And to my family for the pictures and the words.

Karen Solie was born in Moose Jaw and raised in southwest Saskatchewan. Her first collection of poems, *Short Haul Engine,* won the Dorothy Livesay Poetry Prize of the BC Book Prizes and was shortlisted for the Griffin Poetry Prize, the Gerald Lampert Award, and the ReLit Prize. She lives in Toronto.